If your child struggles with a word, you can encourage "sounding it out," but keep in mind that not all words can be sounded out. Your child might pick up clues about a word from the picture, other words in the sentence, or any rhyming patterns. If your child struggles with a word for more than five seconds, it is usually best to simply say the word.

Most of all, remember to praise your child's efforts and keep the reading fun. After you have finished the book, ask a few questions and discuss what you have read together. Rereading this book multiple times may also be helpful for your child.

Try to keep the tips above in mind as you read together, but don't worry about doing everything right. Simply sharing the enjoyment of reading together will increase your child's reading skills and help to start your child off on a lifetime of reading enjoyment!

Sharks!

A We Both Read® Book

This book is dedicated with special thanks to Judith Hunt for all the wonderful illustrations she has created throughout the years.

Special thanks also to John E. McCosker, PhD, Chair of Aquatic Biology, California Academy of Sciences, for his review of the text and his assistance in ensuring the scientific accuracy of this book.

Text Copyright © 2012 by Sindy McKay
Illustrations Copyright © 2012 by Judith Hunt and Wendy Smith

Use of photographs provided by:
Nature Picture Library: 2 Juan Carlos Munoz; 11 Jurgen Freund; 12 Alex Mustard; 15, 32 Jeff Rotman; 16 Doug Perrine; 25t David Tipling, 25b Patricio R Gil; 24, 29 Alan James
National Geographic Images: 3 Mike Parry/Minden Pictures; 17 Paul Nicklen; 20 Norbert Wu/Minden Pictures; 19, 22, 28, 31, 33, 35, 37, 38, 41 Brian J. Skerry; 34 Paul Sutherland; 36 Tim Laman; 40 Chris Newbert/Minden Pictures
Getty Images: 7 Fiona Ayerst/Gallo Images **Fotosearch**: Pgs. 8, 13, 39
Brandon Cole: Pgs. 6, 30 **Dr. Stephen Campana**: Pg. 5

We Both Read® is a trademark of Treasure Bay, Inc.

Published by
Treasure Bay, Inc.
P. O. Box 119
Novato, CA 94948 USA

Printed in Singapore

Library of Congress Catalog Card Number: 2011935125

Hardcover ISBN-13: 978-1-60115-261-9
Paperback ISBN-13: 978-1-60115-262-6

We Both Read® Books
Patent No. 5,957,693

Visit us online at:
www.webothread.com

PR 11-11

WE BOTH READ®

Sharks!

By Sindy McKay

With illustrations by
Judith Hunt and Wendy Smith

TREASURE BAY

Great white shark

Sharks are one of the most beautiful and mysterious animals on Earth. They are also one of the most misunderstood. Many people think they are unintelligent killing machines and fear them, but sharks play a vital role in maintaining the **balance** of our oceans' ecosystems.

Great white shark

Some animals in the sea eat plants. Some, like sharks, eat other animals. This helps keep a **balance**. If all the animals ate only plants, soon there might not be any plants left in the sea!

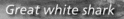

Sharks are fish. Unlike most fish, however, they have no bones. Their skeletons are made of cartilage, the same substance as our ears.

If you rub a shark from head to tail, its skin feels soft. If you rub it from tail to head, its skin feels like very rough sandpaper.

Porbeagle shark and close-up of skin

.004 inches

Photo of porbeagle shark skin by Dr. Steven Campana, Bedford Institute of Oceanography, Canada

A shark's skin is made of many small tooth-like scales. These make the skin of a shark very thick and strong.

Mako shark

   Like all fish, sharks breathe through their gills. Some, such as makos (MAY-koes) and salmon sharks, must force water to flow across their gills by swimming forward with their mouths open. These sharks have to move constantly in order to breathe.

Lemon sharks

Sharks move their body and tail in a side-to-side motion. This propels them through the water.

Reef shark

 There are at least 500 known species of sharks alive today. They come in many shapes and sizes.

Many of them have torpedo-shaped bodies that help them glide through the water at great speeds.

Mako shark

The mako (MAY-koe) shark is very fast. It can also leap up to twenty feet out of the water.

Dwarf lantern shark

One of the smallest sharks is the tiny six-inch dwarf lantern shark. It has an unusual way to camouflage itself from predators below. It produces a glowing light on its underside that blends in with the sunlight coming from above.

Whale shark

The whale shark is the biggest fish in the ocean. Some whale sharks are bigger than a bus!

Angel shark

 Some sharks, such as **wobbegongs** (WOB-ee-gongs) and angel sharks, look like they have been squished down and flattened by a giant iron. This angel shark is well camouflaged as it lies in wait on the sandy bottom of the ocean, ready to surprise its **prey**.

Tasseled wobbegong shark

The patterns on the back of these **wobbegong** (WOB-ee-gong) sharks make them look like plants. They lie very still as their **prey** come near. When the **prey** is very close, the **wobbegong** strikes.

13

Sharks have lived in the waters of our world for over 400 million years. The oldest shark fossils date back to before the age of the dinosaurs. The sharks of today are relatives of these giant animals. One kind of ancient shark that is now extinct was the **megalodon**.

The jaws of a megalodon

This is a model of the jaws and teeth of the **megalodon**. **Megalodon** sharks were more than two times as big as the modern great white shark.

Spiny dogfish

Modern sharks inhabit oceans all around the world. Among the most common are the spiny dogfishes. They prefer the warmer coastal waters of the Pacific and Atlantic Oceans.

Greenland shark

This is a Greenland shark. It likes the much colder waters of the North Atlantic.

Ganges river shark

 While most sharks like the salty waters of the ocean, some sharks live in freshwater rivers. River sharks are primarily found in Australia and Asia. There are five known species of river sharks.

Bull shark

Bull sharks can be found in both oceans *and* rivers. They have even been found in some rivers in America.

Horn shark egg case

A number of sharks give birth to live babies, similar to what humans do. Others lay eggs, like birds do. However, shark eggs don't look much like bird eggs. For example, horn shark eggs look like big screws and are often laid in cracks in a rock.

The shape of a horn shark egg helps to hold it in place. It keeps the egg from floating away in the sea.

Oceanic whitetip shark

All sharks are carnivores. That means they are meat eaters. Some eat krill. Others eat fish, squid, and marine mammals like seals and sea lions. Some sharks will even eat other sharks! Stingrays seem to be a favorite food of some hammerheads.

The hammerhead shark uses its "hammer" like a metal detector. It can detect the electrical pulses of stingrays under the sand.

Basking shark

 The massive basking shark eats some of the smallest animals in the ocean. Every day it must consume huge amounts of tiny krill and plankton.

 Krill are small and shrimp-like. They can be found in every ocean.

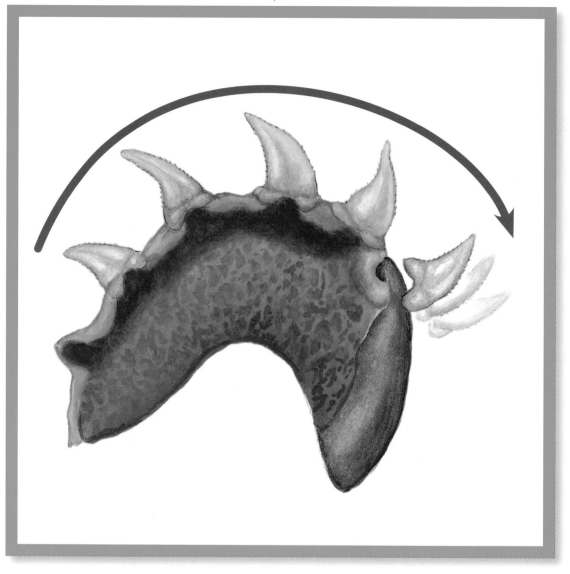

Sharks are one of the most effective predators in the sea. One reason for this is their teeth. Sharks have between five and fifteen rows of teeth. When a front row tooth becomes worn, it falls out and the sharper tooth behind it moves forward to take its place. Sharp teeth are essential for a shark to capture its prey.

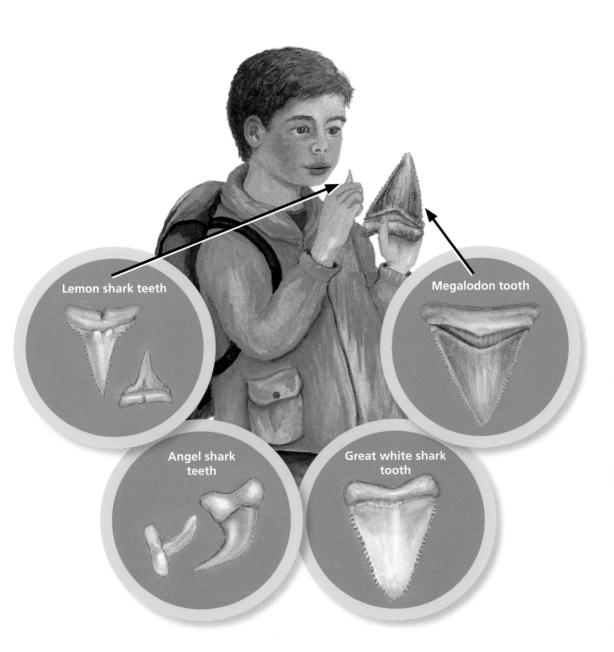

Lemon shark teeth

Megalodon tooth

Angel shark teeth

Great white shark tooth

Shark teeth come in many shapes and sizes.
Different teeth work better to catch different prey.

Oceanic whitetip shark

Another reason sharks are such good predators is their sense of smell. Some sharks can smell blood in the water from almost a quarter of a mile away. They also have good hearing and eyesight.

Whitetip reef sharks

Sharks can see well in dim light. This helps when they are hunting in deep waters or at night.

 All these skills help make sharks the most dreaded creatures in the ocean. They are not only feared by other marine animals but also by **people**. The thought of a shark attack can be terrifying!

Tiger shark

The truth is that shark attacks are rare. Sharks almost never want to bite or eat **people**. They do not like how **people** taste!

There are only about one hundred shark bites reported every year. Very few of these are fatal. You are more likely to be killed by a lightning strike than by a shark bite.

Caribbean reef sharks

There are some people who like to get in the water with sharks. They want to find out more about them.

Marine biologist attaching a transmitter to a tiger shark

Scientists who study sharks have learned that many species are on the verge of extinction. By learning more about them, they hope that they can save these magnificent animals before they disappear forever.

Scientists may use a shark cage when they study sharks. It is a safe way to get close to them.

Red mangrove trees

Researchers have learned that there are three main reasons for the potential extinction of so many shark species. First is loss of habitat, especially the mangrove forests found on tropical coastlines around the world.

Lemon shark pups swimming around mangrove tree roots

 Many shark pups are born in these forests.
The tree roots give them a safe place to hide.

Thresher shark caught in a fishing net

Overfishing for food or sport is another cause for the decline in the number of sharks.

Lastly, thousands are caught in commercial fishing nets meant to catch other kinds of fish. The dead sharks trapped in these nets are simply discarded back into the ocean as trash.

Caribbean reef shark

Fewer than ten people are killed by sharks every year. Millions of sharks are killed by people every year.

School of scalloped hammerhead sharks

 The more we learn about sharks, the more we will be able to put aside our fear of these amazing creatures.

Sharks have managed to survive for over 400 million years.

Caribbean reef sharks

It is up to us to make sure they survive another 400 million years.

If you liked *Sharks!*, here is another
We Both Read® book you are sure to enjoy!

About the Ocean

The ocea   ne ali   fi
the We Bot   d
ph tograph
th   ean
b   oung
to
fa
sh